ALSO BY PATRICK HICKS

The Kingdom of Grass, editor (Center for Western Studies Press, 2010)
Finding the Gossamer (Salmon Poetry, 2008)
The Kiss that Saved My Life (Red Dragonfly Press, 2007)
Draglines (Lone Willow Press, 2006)
Traveling Through History (Moon Pie Press, 2005)
Brian Moore and the Meaning of the Past (Mellen, 2005)

This London
PATRICK HICKS

salmonpoetry

Published in 2010 by
Salmon Poetry
Cliffs of Moher, County Clare, Ireland
Website: www.salmonpoetry.com
Email: info@salmonpoetry.com

Copyright © Patrick Hicks, 2010

ISBN 978-1-907056-27-7

All rights reserved. No part of this publication may be reproduced or transmitted in any form or by any means, electronic or mechanical, including photography, recording, or any information storage or retrieval system, without permission in writing from the publisher. The book is sold subject to the condition that it shall not, by way of trade or otherwise, be lent, resold or otherwise circulated without the publisher's prior consent in any form of binding or cover other than that in which it is published and without a similar condition, including this condition, being imposed on the subsequent purchaser.

Cover artwork: *Building Time* | © *Fabrizio Argonauta* | *Dreamstime.com*
Cover design & typesetting: *Siobhán Hutson*
Printed in England by imprint*digital*.net

…for my mother, Lynne,
who showed me the map

Acknowledgements

Thanks are due to the editors of the following journals in which these poems made early appearances:

Acumen, Ambit, The Baltimore Review, Briar Cliff Review, The Christian Science Monitor, Cold Mountain Review, The Connecticut Review, The Cresset, Descant, Grain, The London Magazine, The Louisville Review, Natural Bridge, The Normal School, Paddlefish, The Powhatan Review, Poet Lore, Poetry East, Tar River Poetry, and *The Writer.*

I am grateful for two ARAF Grants which allowed me to conduct research in London over two summers—without such financial help this book would not have been possible. Special thanks to the Mikkelsen Library for commissioning "Library of the Mind" for a dedication ceremony; this poem later transformed itself into "Outside the British Library".

The list of people I need to thank for their friendship and encouragement is long but I want to express my gratitude to Nick Hayes, Tricia Currans-Sheehan, Jim Reese, Christine Stewart-Nuñez, Jessie Lendennie, Eamonn Wall, Jeanne Emmons, Sheila Risacher, Erin Crowder, Jim Hicks, Jayson Funke, the late Bill Holm, the English Department at Augustana College, and the good monks at Saint John's University. I'm absolutely beholden to Brian Turner and David Allan Evans for their critiques of the early manuscript (thanks gentlemen). Above all others, I offer my continued thanks to Tania for her patience, love, and understanding...not many wives would allow their husband to disappear into London for as long as I did. Thanks for letting me get on those airplanes, Tania, and for much, *much* more.

Contents

Nursery of Words . . . 11

Zone 1

After the First Performance of *Hamlet* . . . 15
At the Globe with Shakespeare . . . 16
New London, Minnesota . . . 17
Piccadilly Circus at Night . . . 18
Scratching My Eye . . . 19
The Poet of Liverpool Street Station . . . 20
London Underground . . . 21
Riding the Tube . . . 22
Riding the Tube after the Bombings . . . 23
Burqa . . . 24

Zone 2

Dictionary . . . 27
City of Words . . . 28
Study Abroad Assignment at the British Museum . . . 29
Taste of India . . . 30
At the Pub . . . 31
Battersea Power Station . . . 32
Bedlam . . . 34
At the Gallows of Tyburn . . . 36
Breakfast with the Dead . . . 37

Zone 3

Where Oscar Wilde is Not Buried . . . 41
While Strolling Through Highgate Cemetery,
    I Consider the Morning of My Own Funeral . . . 42
In Hades . . . 43

What I Have Learned After 37 Years	44
Lighting the Christmas Tree	45
The Lady with the Lamp	46
In Peace	47
Generations after the Plague	50
The Great Stink of 1858	51
The Knowledge	52
To My Hands	54

Zone 4

London Burning	57
Infamous	60
Red Light District	61
Climbing Boys	62
The Forgotten	63

Zones 5–6

To the Woman Feeding Squirrels	67
Halal Delicatessen	68
Chinatown	69
Thinking of My Wife in South Dakota	70
Fatality on the Tracks	71
At Buckingham Palace, I think of Jon M	72
Meeting Terri for Lunch	73
Letter to James Joyce	74
The Same is Different Every Day	75
Taking Photographs for Strangers	76
Outside the British Library	77
Note to a Friend Yet to be Born	78
Love Song	79

Notes 81

Biography 87

Nursery of Words

"Oh God! It's all over."
—Frederick North, British Prime Minister,
on learning about the surrender at Yorktown, 1781

In spite of my thinned Irish blood
and that battle in Virginia,

I have returned with the flag of a pen
to claim these streets as my own.

Two hundred years of imperial rule
lies in the muck of Jamestown,

but this city was once my capital—
this backwater outpost of Rome.

In this nursery of words, and gunpowder,
my hyphenated tongue begins to twitch.

ZONE 1

*"This happy breed of men, this little world,
this precious stone set in the silver sea ...
this blessed plot, this earth, this realm, this England."*

—William Shakespeare

After the First Performance of *Hamlet*

Who's there?
Nay, answer me.

And so, the words are born into a globe of ears
even though the skull has yet to be lifted from the grave,
the "to be" is still not to be, and the ending is anyone's guess.

These few, the lucky ones who felt like catching a show today,
cannot imagine they have stumbled into a nursery
where characters are given voice for the very first time.

These witnesses hold their bladders and pence and oranges
while, up the street, executioners and whores are busy with bodies,
the queen sits down to lunch, and the Thames unspools into the sea.

London is unaware that the defining words of their age are,
at this very moment, ribboning from an actor's mouth—
what matters to history often astonishes those living through it.

On the stage, as Hamlet coils anger around a blade,
no one realises that he is tossing words into the future.
In fact, long after this day has curtained to a close,

the box office counted on a lost wooden table,
and the actors' throats cooled with pints of beer,
the stage will be emptied, the doors padlocked shut,

and everyone, including Shakespeare,
will go to bed believing that just another day
has changed costume into night.

At the Globe with Shakespeare

What would he make of our metal birds in the sky,
the large ones that rumble smoky plumage?
What would he say about our living tapestries,
those things we call "movies" and "television"?
Would he listen to Mozart or the Beatles?
His earring would still be *en vogue*,
so too his long hair. His ruff,
however, would have to go.
His speech would be of interest to linguists,
and he would surely applaud
the printing press on everyone's desk,
but if he could watch his plays, here,
what stage directions would he give?
Maybe he would rather read
about the development of drama,
sip a latte, then scout across
the borderlands of the dispossessed.
There he would take out his notepad,
marvel briefly at the ball-point pen,
and he would begin to scribble,
his cell phone turned off, his ears open,
his hand fluttering like mad.

New London, Minnesota

Who came to bust sod
and lumberjack these trees into buildings?
Why did they choose this name for their town,
a place so deep and landlocked in the prairie?
In this London, a cowboy store sells
lutefisk, moose statues, and moccasins.
The Riverside Café in this riverless town
has an *Olde Ice-cream Shoppe*,
which at least recalls some version of England.
Out here, waffle cones and sundaes
are claimed by little American flags
on toothpicks.

None of this matters
to the old farmer getting out of his pickup,
his John Deere baseball cap speckled with mud.
This withered gentleman of New London uses a cane,
he squints at a parody of Big Ben, a grain elevator,
one that holds a parliament of corn.
Silence walks down the street on manure-tanged air.
A pond, pocked with waterlilies and bullfrogs,
wears a crown of trees, a veil of butterflies.

Prairiegrass sways in the heat,
a hissing whispering ocean.

The clouds above these streets
will soon sail across the Atlantic,
chart a course for the namesake of this town,
and unload a harvest of rain.

How strange,
because tomorrow I will board a plane
and plant my feet in the mighty city
that seeded this place.

Under that enormous clockface,
I will lift my eyes like a corn shoot.

17

Piccadilly Circus at Night

Red doubledeckers gear around us
as two punks jitterbug in the corner,
their kilts and green hair are supernovas.
Everyone here absorbs neon and gravity,
we pulse into the ventricle of the city.
Thousands rivercomet past us,
they pole themselves forward with cameras,

dipping the shutter,
snagging light
one frame at a time.

This is a kingdom for the eyes.
Everyone takes photos, proof
that we inhaled the fireworking bulbs.

I walk in liquid sparks,
knowing that I am just a prop
in someone else's photograph.
And yet it proves that I, too,
moved through the world—
my little star burned for a moment,
then winked out.

Scratching My Eye

As I rubbed a finger
              across my eye,
a thorn of glass
sliced open my world.

Now, glittering lights
bleed
as if underwater.

I worry about
doublevision,
cornea damage,
blackness.

Everything looks new.

It was glass that hurt me
and it will be glass,
          those spider eyes of a phoropter,
that will heal me.

I can already hear
my optometrist asking the wall:
is this better, or this?

Until then, I squint through rain
and wonder if the world's hummingbird speed
will ever look the same again.

The Poet of Liverpool Street Station

The Elephant Man grazed here,
cloak open to reveal his bloated skeleton.
Over the years, the steam engine soot has thinned,
but the lumbering ghost of this famous sideshow
still begs our attention, his one good eye
bent sideways, the tusk of his pen
rooting for poems of love.

With the trunk of his tongue,
Joseph Merrick sniffs words,
he aches to rewrite his pachyderm body,
his thickened skull is ready to unforget
the gasps of women and children.

He pinches pennies while, hooded,
he sways away beneath gas lamps,
limping now for the graveyard of his flat,
for the paper, and the ink, and the silence.

Who better than a poet could understand
the cutting power of words,
the blunderbuss of such lethal insults?

London Underground

Piped in steel,
your murky secrets run beneath the street—
Beverley Brook, Ravensbourne, Wandle.
Cooled iron and bolts, your clamped hospice.
Skiffs once poled through the silt of your inlets,
but now even the wide Fleet gushes
unseen beneath a sheet of asphalt.
An old viaduct, a mocking crown,
coronates your stolen riverbanks.
Sunlight no longer jewels your surface,
molluscs do not limp through your mud,
and dolphins are a murky memory.
Standing here in Sloane Square,
waiting for the District Line tube,
what is left of the Westbourne babbles
blindly through overhead ducting.
Both of us are herded by Charon,
carried forward, denied the mothy
shimmer of moonlight, we share
the flow of a tightening O,
a pipe that hurtles us beneath the city,
pennies bolted over our eyes.

Riding the Tube

> *Mind   the gap*
> *Mind   the gap*
> *Mind*

the blindness   between stations
the railed void   between
departure   and arrival
the platform   we leave behind

as we journey   ahead:
Chalk Farm   to Covent Garden
Whitechapel   to Blackfriars
Bank   to Angel

the abandoned   objects
on these trains   is a tunnelling
between lost   and found:

cell phones, an urn of ashes, a false eye, breast
implants, a jug of bull's sperm, umbrellas,
2 human heads, a ventriloquist's dummy, teeth,
a vasectomy kit, lecture notes on John Donne,
bitten apples, empty wallets, divorce papers, blood,

us, not minding   the gaps,
our little hearts   thumping
like trains   between

now // and now // and now // and now // and

Riding the Tube after the Bombings

July 9, 2005

The doors squeeze us together,
and our fear tightens,
like a winter belt.

Russell Square

In spite of those angry suicides,
rush hour continues,
deep beneath these streets.

Holborn

I glance around,
and guard the city
of my organs.

Covent Garden

Nazi bombs and Irish blasts
should be ancient history today

Leicester Square

and yet, these old explosions
feel closer than ever before—
their fire blisters my skin

Piccadilly Circus

in this webbing of tunnels,
and time, we tingle with fear.
Each second is a detonation.

Burqa

> *"Patriotism is not enough,*
> *I must have no hatred or bitterness for anyone."*
> —Edith Cavell

A waterfall of people trickled down the stairs
and she, beneath a burqa that was flinty,
full of sparks, positioned her stroller

at the top.
The front wheels clunked
like stones towards the station below.

Wordlessly, I unstopped myself
and took the front struts in both hands.
Together, we carried her boy towards the ground—
all of us were once this small,
our bones this soft and compact.

The rectangle of her eyes squinted a smile,
and when I looked back, she waved.

Zone 2

"When a man is tired of London, he is tired of life."

—Samuel Johnson

Dictionary n.f. [*dictionarium*, Latin.] **1.** A book holding words of any language in alphabetical order; **2.** a lexicon; **3.** a word pool that mirrors social thought.

Back during the gin craze of the 1700s,
when colonial bounty was stacked across London,
Samuel Johnson felt words flow around him.
His bulk, like an O, buoyed him in pubs and palaces,
syllables broke against the gunwale of his ear.

A book was planned, and his *amanuenses*
(they entered that word on page three),
flapped open a great net of ink.-
Johnson hunched at his desk like a C
and sorted speech into kingdoms.
For years he stood like a Y directing traffic,
shepherding words into their stalls,
everything from *aardvark* to *zebu*.

When Johnson's great ship of a book
was finally launched into public thought,
his black manservant, Frank Barber,
picked up the Middle Passage of words
that he had helped to quill.
He looked up words like *empire*
and *independence* and *slave*.

This freeman knew the power of connotation,
he stood as rigid and as proper as a capital I,
and he insisted that the word *abolition* be included,
so that the world could see it, chained onto page one.

City of Words

It started when Brutus herded cows
through the mudflats of Tamesis.
That word, for it is words that build walls,
was crushed beneath the roads of Londinium.
After Nero's plucking, the Anglo-Saxons
rowed upstream, flexed their accents,
split mighty oaks into walls, created Lundenwíc.
Decades of vowel-chewing made it Lundenburg,
followed by French bricks of sound until—
now—young immigrants spice the pronunciation
of Leicester Square, Southwark, and Marylebone.
It isn't just history that stamps citizenship,
but the tongue, and the ear.

Study Abroad Assignment at the British Museum

When I shepherd students into London,
I always bring them to this museum
and tell them to find something British.
The bright ones realise I am a god of trickery,
that this is a warehouse of colonial plunder.

"So what makes a nation, a nation?" I ask.
The words that open our mouths only go so far,
flags shed their colour in time,
history is a book of quicksand,
    borders move.

It's best not to consider that foreign countries
are tidal rivers, as muddy as our own,
full of whirlpools and evolving creatures.
So it is easier to ask a security guard,
"what's British in the British Museum?"

She lifts an eyebrow and scratches
the corn-rows of her hair.
In a Jamaican accent, she says,
"Most people visit the Rosetta Stone…
I guess that's British enough."

It is a start,
but that slab of granite was stolen
from a village now called el-Rashid.
That skeleton key of language makes us believe
we can translate history, that it's only a stream
we can sleepwalk over as easily as catching a plane
across the Atlantic, resetting our watches,
and landing safely in a new time zone.

We open the book of our passport,
trusting that it can interpret the land,
but the marks that spell out our names
are just little hieroglyphics, waving in the heat.

Taste of India

Vindaloo is blacksmithing my mouth
even though, again and again,
I have doused it with beer.

Lava bubbles in my gut,
my tongue is a lump of coal.
Any minute now,
I will burst into flame.

We white faces work our plates
while the grandsons of former colonials
look on, grinning, tallying what we owe—

tip not included.

At the Pub

Like goatskin over a drum,
their football jerseys strain
against swollen beer bellies.
These lads yell stadium anthems,
they thump the floor, ready for war.
Empty pint glasses stud the table.
Tattoos, those inky badges of belonging,
stitch their forearms together.
These men are a ring of flesh,
as immovable as Stonehenge.
But tonight, after last call,
they will count pennies
and answer to their wives.

Battersea Power Station

October 1997

Pink Floyd made it famous with an album cover,
and when I see it, I think of flying pigs.

But there is also that party in Chelsea,
the one where I smoked my last joint ~
      when something else burrowed into my lungs.

My hands dripped. My heart was a hand grenade.
It exploded, and exploded, and exploded, so oddly
that my buddy, a cardiologist, also high,
thought I was going into "V-Tach",
which is what he screamed into the phone.

The world became a sprint, vaguely,
as from beneath syrup and liquid lampposts
Battersea Power Station galloped next to the ambulance,
snorkelling the night.

I thought of putting coins in my eyes, waiting
for the devil to open the back of the meatwagon,
his red mouth
         and teeth
swallowing me, like a pill.

Instead, a doctor from Iraq took my pulse,
he placed his holy hand on my forehead
and pronounced me alive.

His lips were neon butterflies.
"Relax. You've taken a hallucinogen."

•

The next morning
I climbed into a blue sober day
and walked near Battersea.

The chimneys of the old power station
looked like an inverted gurney.

I moved away, bending with the river,
never feeling so alive, so wired with current.

Bedlam

I. Royal Hospital for the Insane

Epileptics, homosexuals, and the deformed
were stored here, put on public display,
their tongues straight-jacketed.

Little girls were dumped here after being raped.
The name of this place is a corruption of "Bethlehem"—
and so it should be, innocence was murdered here.

Each dawn, the insane shuffled around the courtyard:
      Napoleon plotting his escape,
        Christ waiting for the spikes and the lifting,
      girls clawing away from their cocked guards.

When Bedlam shut its doors,
sunlight shafted through the windows,
it warmed strange metal flowers,
the open petals of iron leggings and neck shackles.

Chains, like creeper, were rooted to the floor.

This garden of evil was still fresh with sin
so a padlock was fitted to the front gate,
locking out the world, or maybe
locking it in.

II. Imperial War Museum

Panzers and Jeeps form a ring of weaponry,
the madness of the 20th-Century is shackled near a gift shop.
In the basement of this old warehouse for the insane,
rifles peek over sandbags, speakers thud out explosions,
a vent pumps in the stink of mouldy potatoes. Zig-
zagging through this mock trench, it is 1916 again.
Epoxy mud covers the wall, bayonets are flimsy,
the ground is dry, and the Germans are just little toys,
illuminated cottonballs crack open their deaths.
Near the exit, three mannequins huddle over a gun.
They ready themselves for a charge into no-man's-land
which will begin in…3, 2, 1

a whistle pierces the dry ice
"Now! Now! Quick, boys!"

                In my imagination
these soldiers march into an abyss of steel.

I want to break their guns, push them outside
where they can throw down their helmets,
but the audio tape rewinds,
and these soldiers are dragged back in time,
cruelly resurrected. The tape clicks on
and they die again, and again,
and again, and again.

At the Gallows of Tyburn

anytime during the 1700s

Back then, shoving through a drunken crush of people,
it was a two-hour parade from Newgate Prison
to the hanging tree. For the condemned,
swallowing must have felt like a newborn miracle.
They must have caressed the strange fruit of their Adam's apple,
the words of tomorrow, wedged in their throats.

Then the heavy noose, the quick drop and that sudden
snap. Your feet kicking at death, a face swollen with blood,
the purse of your neck cinched shut—but your ears,

your ears are wide open.

Breakfast with the Dead

Double-decker buses drumroll past the Tyburn Café,
which has the best breakfast in all of London:
*bacon, fried bread, eggs (your choice), potato wedge,
mushrooms, blood pudding   all under £3*

Thousands had their necks pulled near this espresso machine,
just across from that display of muffins,
but waiters flit now through falling ghosts.
The dead rise up through linoleum,
they unloop the noose, massage their cinched throats.

I sip coffee amid this parade of dead women,
soot-dusted chimneysweep boys,
gentlemen in buckled shoes
—the collar of a bruise around every neck—
most of them dangled for petty crime.

No monument stands where they fell.
There is only Connaught House, on the corner,
the name reminds me of bony bodies
                    dropping

into the blighted clachans of Ireland.
Such is the way of memory and history,
the long-dead are easily forgotten to us.
I eat yolk and am thankful for a tongue

that has never known the word "famine",
for a neck that does not fear the hanging tree.
The morning sun heats my table,
the world shimmers in leafy molten gold.

My stomach works on a potato while my fellow dinners
nibble toast, sip orange juice, our healthy throats open and close.

We pat the filled drum of our stomachs and gaze into the future
where, centuries from now, we too will have dropped

                                  into the earth.

That's when we ask the dead around us to pull up a chair,
take a load off—they sit and breathe the incense of our coffee.
Who knew that heaven had a menu or that God was a
    short-order cook,
his checkered apron tied around his belly, he holds a spatula

and prepares everyone's favourite meal—
yoghurt for the Hindus sitting at the counter,
kosher and halal beef for table number five,
a cup of silence for the Buddhists.

The *ding-ding* of his order-up bell
drowns out the shouts of world history,
he comes forth, revealing himself at last.

As he dismantles the clock above the door,
everyone at this old execution ground,
the living and the dead,
begins to cheer, full throated, alive,
our mugs of bottomless coffee raised in the air,
our steam and voices lifting together as one.

Zone 3

"The man who can dominate a London dinner-table can dominate the world."

—Oscar Wilde

Where Oscar Wilde is Not Buried

Highgate Cemetery is shrouded in leaves,
wild saplings sprout from bodies that once ruled London.
These wealthy Victorians now stew in the dark,
        they rot in a web of earthworms.
But they once strolled through the tarry fog of night,
they once listened to gas lamps hiss like will-o-the-wisps.

Oscar isn't buried with the likes of them.
No, he's in that other necropolis, Père-Lachaise,
where artists dip their brushes into the neon of Paris,
writers use the ink of night, Chopin bangs the piano
and Jim Morrison lines up shots of absinthe.
All these old lives unshoulder the dirt together
while fountains of champagne firework the sky.

In Père-Lachaise, kisses flutter around the tomb of Oscar Wilde,
these lipstick butterflies open their wings on the forehead
of his sepulchre, offering the graffiti of respect.
Maybe—maybe at this very moment—
someone is pressing their warm lips against Oscar's tomb,
thanking him for the words that once rose from his mouth.

He should really be in London though,
in the city that made and unmade him.
If only that "sodomite and home wrecker"
were in the boneyard of Highgate Cemetery,
he'd bring legions of feet to trample the earth.
Like gatecrashers, those kisses
would remind the dead they sent Oscar packing.

If he were in Highgate Cemetery tonight
his sardonic cool would nudge those prudes,
he'd knock the coins from their eyes,
he'd shake the mud from their joints.

And then,
while smoking a cigarette without fear of getting cancer,
he'd announce that one must live well,
        especially in death.

While Strolling Through Highgate Cemetery, I Consider the Morning of My Own Funeral

It should be cool, overcast,
and the birds should be silent,
except for the crows. My friends,
as you dress yourselves in black
and make your way to the steeple,
to glowing walls of stained glass,
to the living orchids and beetles and
the heavy bounty of yet another day,
I'd like to hear your memories of me,
especially the ones I've forgotten.

Go ahead and cry a little,
I think I'd like a few tears.
As far as music is concerned,
I want something joyous and lively.
My Irish blood, even in congealed death,
is aching for a good romp up the aisle.
So let the uilleann skip a bright and ancient birdsong,
one that plucks me from the casket,
and makes me boogie into the cloudless vast
where I will hang, briefly, like an ellipsis…

If you want to know where I am hiding,
where my spirit has gone, I am the grace notes
that you place between these words.

If you miss me, read this again,
and like Lazarus, I will come forth.

In Hades

The dead measure us, steely eyed,
from their pedestals around this city—
Churchill pulls on an iron cigar,
a wounded admiral stands in a crow's nest,
Queen Victoria sits in a chiselled chair.
These statues envy the traffic of our blood,
and our ability to shoo away pigeons.

Moving through this underworld,
easily crisscrossing the Thames,
there is no hooded boatman for us.
We can escape the grey rain,
we can glide through sunlight,
our limbs swaying, unbound,

effortlessly alive.

What I Have Learned After 37 Years

In the morning, when I stumble into the world, wooden floor slats fit my feet like skis. Outside, robins pluck trumpets, crickets rub their ukulele legs together. The foggy dawn hides the sun, it weaves the grass into a beaded quilt. The coffee beans are within reach and I am still here, breathing. After 37 years, I have learned never to love a day more than this one.

Lighting the Christmas Tree

Trafalgar Square

The Big Bang also needed a spark,
a fuse to get the galaxies going.
Long after the fiery birth of our universe,
a raging star imploded one day,

spewing itself back into the cosmos

so that, as the story goes,
three wise men might find their way
through the desert towards a new halo.
From light we began, and to light we will return.

We can't imagine a time before time began,
back when light was still only an idea, an unlit bulb.
And so, beneath the stars, we wait for the plug and socket,
for a spark to split the darkness wide open.

The Lady with the Lamp

No matter what Tennyson had to say about it,
you knew the charge of the Light Brigade
was just an un-poetic spray of blood.
I see you unrolling miles of gauze
and swaddling the wounded at Scutari,
you lift their snapped bodies into sunlight.

I almost love you, Miss Nightingale,
for going to war against war,
and when you came home to London,
you cut through soaking red tape.
You could have married a mansion
and spent your days in a rose garden,

        but instead,
you hammered your lamp
to the rafters of a hospital system.

I love the borderless country of your heart.

You spent your final days curdling in bed,
still dictating orders that might heal shattered bones,
mouldy skin, and blackened stumps of meat.

With only hours to live, you wanted more candles
so that you might work deep into the night.

From the street, your little lamp flickered on,
a flame, twitching restlessly in the dark.

In Peace

I. At the Grave of the Unknown Warrior

Westminster Abbey

Your name is buried in French soil,
melted bullets spell out your right
to be interred among poets and kings.
You died anonymous and young,
but a fellow trenchmate, now 111 years old,
will be buried next to you when he fades away.
A type of alpha and omega—side by side.

What must it be like for this last witness of the Great War,
his mind gummed with colour images
of what he saw at the Somme and Ypres?
When this old soldier is finally laid to rest,
more than his life will be taken from the earth.
The last living memory of a war born in 1914
will be hushed in the dark, lidded with stone.

It was like this for Gettysburg and Waterloo,
or when they buried the oldest of Shakespeare's friends.
Someone too was the last person to remember Golgotha,
how the sun was shining that day,
how the body slumped towards the ground.

II. Seeing the Great War at Charing Cross Station

It is 2007 today, but it feels more like 1917.
Squinting through a kaleidoscope of history,
an army is here, rifles slung over their knapsacks,
they are spun towards no-man's-land.

These soldiers walk on healthy legs,
they have yet to be baptised by the oil of war.
Women cheer them off into a termite existence,
where they will become little wasps
caught in pus, and mud, and bones.

Kisses are blown,
like from that blonde over there,
the one next to *Delice de France*—a pastry shop
that sells croissants dripping with the blood of jam.

I watch her boyfriend, dressed in a trenchcoat,
step into a train, waving.

His hand is swallowed from view
and he is gone,
simply gone.

III. D-Day + 64 Years

Imperial War Museum

Busloads of teenagers surround me.
They lift their eyes into that day of fireclouds,
when the tide drowned in bodies of men.

Dressed in school uniforms,
armed with pencils, they take notes,
and rummage through backpacks for chocolate.

What can this possibly mean to the students
who stroll around me, flirting, laughing, breathing?

A young man stands near a map.
He presses his whole giant hand
across the beaches of Utah, Omaha,
Gold, Juno, and Sword.

He says, in a type of hush,
"so *that's* where he died."

Generations after the Plague

Death infested this city of organs,
it gummed lungs with phlegm,
and nibbled flesh to the reeking bone.
Quicklime couldn't work fast enough,
horses plodded to pits, driverless.
Carts of liquefying flesh, crucifixes,
pockets-full-of-posies, and yellowed eyes,
all tumbled into the maggoty dark.
Grass grew tall in the marketplace.

Silence woke up, surprised.

•

Today, beneath sandals and designer shoes,
the plague naps on leathery limbs.
Up from jackhammers and blowtorches
the dead rise like bony weeds,
their mouths open, exhaling.

Biohazard-suits lift those who all fell down,
making way for water pipes and computer lines,
they slice through this shale of poisonous bone.
The limbs of these premature resurrectants
are acid-cleansed beneath fluorescent lights,
they are placed in shoeboxes, sealed in a museum vault.

From their paper coffins
these souls contemplate their lifting.
They are puzzled by Judgement Day.
Where is Gabriel and his horn?
The thundering horses? The promise of wings?
Is this heaven beneath the sodium lights?

The Great Stink of 1858

"It is a Stygian pool reeking with ineffable and unbearable horror."
—Benjamin Disraeli

Simmering thickly beneath a July sun,
the Thames was soupy excrement.
London bathed drapes in horse urine,
wore masks doused in *eau de toilette*,
but still the sour fog seeped
into homes, food, and throats.
Monsters, it was believed,
lived in the unholy perfume,
their razor teeth rutted cholera,
they backstroked through veins,
and grew fat on children's souls.
In that summer of egg rotten air,
the river was a damp corpse,
everyone survived on barrels of beer.

Today, sitting in a riverside pub,
      a wet pint in my hand,
I offer a toast to breathable air,
to city engineers, to modern hygiene,
to lungs buoyant with laughter, to small problems,
to the angels that flutter down my throat,
they dance now, gulp after cleansing gulp.

The Knowledge

"I began to study the plan of London ... it is impossible ever to become thoroughly acquainted with such an endless labyrinth."
—Robert Southey

It all started when a man lashed
his horse down a weedy footpath.

Then wagons roamed towards brothels
and the temple of Mithras.

From dray to hackney-cab,
a parade of vehicles drove

wheel ruts into stone.
Two millennia later,

our taxis move slower
than Roman charioteers.

Hear them lift the lash
of their voice, bellowing

for movement, darting
like fish down side streets.

Rumour has it that taxi drivers
develop a larger hippocampus

so they can learn "the knowledge"—
such is the webbed calculus

of London's many streets.
How odd to hold these pathways,

these neurons of asphalt,
in the map of your mind.

What is it like to flick down
the fare meter, push out your chin,

and head into the labyrinth undaunted?
There, between your hands, the city unrolls

as if it were still just a one-horse town.

To My Hands

Even before you punched the womb
and thrummed the umbilical cord,
I have taken you for granted,
yet you hang before me, obedient as puppets.
True, I have scribbled notes on you,
cut and burnt you badly, but the day will come
when the ponds in your knuckles will swell,
slowing us both.

But, hands, I want to thank you now
for the adventures we have shared:
how you have fluttered neckties into shape,
burrowed for names in a phonebook,
tap danced across the stage of a keyboard.
Let's not forget about our long walks across naked bodies,
or that time you tried to feed me with chopsticks.

So thank you for pointing at shooting stars,
for waiting on the street corner of a page,
and opening the locked doors of night.
No wonder each of your fingers has a halo.

The day of your retirement will come,
when we will both sit in a wheelchair.
You will be twisted with arthritis,
and I will look upon you,
asleep in the hammock of my lap,
thankful for your service,
understanding, I hope,
that you finally deserve a rest.

Zone 4

"This melancholy London... I sometimes imagine that the souls of the lost are compelled to walk through its streets perpetually. One feels them passing like a whiff of air."

—W. B. Yeats

London Burning

I. Boudicca

> *Londinium, 60 AD*

When her man, King Prasutagus,
finally breathed out his ghost,
the Romans groped her inheritance
and raped her daughters while she watched,
    clear-eyed, unflinching,
even as the whip cut into her back.

Vengeance like hers
should not be banished into the wild.

She returned to Londinium
with 100,000 warriors bent on bloodlust,
and made a pyre of Caesar's colony.
She blinded the dawn with flame.

Surrounded by burnt ribcages
and a wilderness of the freshly crucified,
Boudicca stood there—arms crossed—
sniffing the embers, daring the Romans
to ever touch her daughters again.

II. Inferno

> *"Pah! A woman might piss it out!"*
> —Lord Mayor Thomas Bludworth, 1666

When that hotheaded mayor
was told about a fire in Pudding Lane,
sparks shot from his mouth,
and he went back to sleep.

The night churned with flame,
but by then, anyone with a full bladder
was long gone.

Three days later, the fire laughed
at leaking hand-pumps—
foundation stones glowed white,
lead windowpanes dripped into the streets.
The city became a field of ash.

    Today, a riverbreeze strokes my hair
and it's hard to imagine this hurricane of fire.
Between canyons of steel, I eat a sandwich,
while sunlight lounges on my forearm.

In this lane,
I watch mothers scoop up their children,
and run away from what only I can see.

Around me, the city blazes
while I sit,
smoking a cigarette.

III. Resurgam

> "Is Saint Paul's still standing?"
> —Winston Churchill, 1940

          A broken grave
became its foundation stone—
the Latin word for *Resurrection*
was chiselled into living lichen.
Saint Paul's, wombed in scaffolding,
grew wide above the charred lumber.
This domed heart of London,
coal-stained, beating the years,
was proof of permanence and empire

         until the Luftwaffe
swarmed overhead, their pistons firing,
their bellies swollen with explosives,
the air was thick with swastikas

         searchlights
cut through the droning dark.
A spark rekindled Pudding Lane,
hoses went dry, bricks burst,
the inferno was a premature sunrise,
a forged dawn.

The next morning,
a bellied politician held his cigar
as if he were keeping fire on a leash.

He strolled through rubble,
held aloft two tobacco-stained fingers,
little realising the word *Resurgam*
was hidden deep inside Saint Paul's Cathedral,
that for two millennia this little flower
has been pushing up through layers of ash.

Infamous

Whitechapel, 1888

Death sipped whiskey at the Ten Bells,
in his satchel, knives held darkness.
He watched prostitutes flirt,
their teats on display,
their bloodswollen organs
jiggling darkly in sin.

He aches to make a volcano of their guts.

Look now,
one of them steps into an alleyway,
his knife goes
          slashing
into her marrow,
blade sawing-sawing-sawing
through rubbery vocal cords,
her womb is slooped out—
the wet oyster of her ribcage shimmers—
then he, the Ripper, crushes
the pumping pearl of her heart.

Somewhere in the distance,
a nickelodeon grinds brittle music.

He cleans the blade on her skirt,
then walks away, as mysterious as coal smoke.

Red Light District

The streets of Soho throbbed in an orgasm of light,
so your question shouldn't have surprised me.
Your accent was Russian, born beneath Soviet wreckage,
and I couldn't help but notice the thin fabric of your shirt,
how you were just out of girlhood, on your own.

Huntress, your eyes held me.
I see now that you were out for the kill,
fingers of menstrual blood
        smeared across your cheeks,
betrayal locked in the zoo of your ribcage,
it prowls your heart, sniffing
for the meat of my wallet.

Little daughter, what brought you to London
because, surely, it couldn't be for this,
to slide open your body like a button,
to swing the blunt hammer of this question:
I'm clean ... want to fuck?

Climbing Boys

In the Victorian Age,
orphans were sent up
chimney flues.
Their willowy bodies
would knock out the soot
of family evenings.
Fires were lit
beneath their toes…
and they were forced
to claw the darkness
for that pinhole of light,
which was always
just out of reach,
high above.

The Forgotten

In stockyards, they were rounded up, tagged,
their gold thrown into a blast furnace.
These moneylenders were driven out in 1290,
their strongboxes splintered open with axes.

As churchbells waved a thunderous goodbye,
these Londoners were kicked to the shoreline.
A sword tip in their eye, their children tarred in mud,
they waded into boats, and watched their home

shrink away. I see them vanish from the record
and want to throw them a line. Out go these words,
and I begin to pull.

Zones 5-6

"Always, from the first time he went there to see Eros and the lights, that circus have a magnet for him, that circus represent life, that circus is the beginning and ending of the world."

—Sam Selvon

To the Woman Feeding Squirrels

You are a statue in Saint James's Park,
the gold of a peanut tweaked between finger and thumb.
A low fence holds a squirrel, his tail coiled
into a question mark, fluttering.

When he takes the gift, you reach for another,
as slow as melting ice in November,
you hold it to his nose.

Children scuttle up to watch,
their voices light with wonder,
but you are perfectly still,
oak has filled your veins,
you wiggle the peanut,
cooing a mothersong.
This must be what God is like,
a full bag of nectar caught at his waist.

Slowly,
the squirrel perches in your hand
and there is only this—
you, a needy creature,
and everyone joined together

waiting

Halal Delicatessen

The owner who made my falafel was gruff,
my smile and small talk lost in a desert.
But when his son, speaking a language I did not know,
came around the counter and tugged my jeans,
I gave him my full attention.
He pointed at meat and salad,
saying the words that made them real.

I got down on one knee and pointed at trays,
which brought a feast of words to his lips.
He reached for my hand,
and tugged me into his kingdom.
Diced apples became *tofah*, bread was *khobez*,
he pointed at ice cream, *helu*, and his eyes bloomed.

If only it were this easy, always.

I thought of him as a grown man, oblivious
to this moment of him that I will carry.
Later, we might pass each other on the street,
but today, I am the anchor of his universe.

His father wrapped my sandwich and, pausing,
passed two bottles of water into my hands.
"Hot today. You take these."

His son looked on and pointed, *ma'a*,
he said, *ma'a*, of which we are all made.

Chinatown

for my daughter, who has yet to meet me

Words are boxy hash-marks,
like shrubs in an open field.
Within these pagoda gates
the world is gold and red,
restaurants bubble with duck,
grandmothers carry crates of eggroll.
This foreign world
is giving me an adopted daughter.
I want to sing her name
and learn the grammar of her heart.
She was born in the Middle Kingdom,
but will grow up in South Dakota
where she will play in cornfields
with my wife.

At least we can bring her here,
where our cultural histories meet,
where egg-foo-yung steams near hamburgers.
In this place, we can sit at a table,
and eat our way towards double happiness.

Thinking of My Wife in South Dakota

*"I came to London. It had become the centre of my world
and I had worked hard to come to it. And I was lost."*

—V.S. Naipaul

What must it be like for her,
an immigrant from England,
to know that I am in her country,
not far from the X of her birth?

No wonder she tends peppers,
raises herb gardens, pinches tomatoes.
It is, perhaps, a way for her to make
the land of our backyard her own.

This woman from Devon,
      sunbonnet tucked down over her eyes,
passes a watering-can over swelling vegetables,
ones that stretch away from the American dirt.

When we eat them with butter,
they will be wild, and sweet,
and hers, utterly hers.

Fatality on the Tracks

Victoria Station

We were waiting for our journey to Point B
when the conductor, in blunt words,
told us our train had been cancelled.
*There has been a fatality on the tracks,
please move to Platform 4.*

I thought of greased rails,
unstoppable metal,
eyes widening,
and the impact of a funeral.

But the lady next to me,
with her shopping bags and stormy hair,
was equally destructive when she yelled,
Bloody Hell! Now I'm going to be late!

Molten steel fills my ribcage,
my teeth are barbed-wire,
but the killer bees I want to spit
are stuck on the flypaper of my tongue.

Already, she is picking up steam for the exit.
A cane holding up a man is knocked aside,
and this woman, her bags clattering behind,
explodes down the platform,
the horn of her mouth blaring.

There is an empty moment in the car,
the old man stiffens his suitcoat,
and, in her wake, we are all dragged to Platform 4.
Our bodies are balloons of blood,
so soft, just flesh and eggshell bones.

The hard woman stands alone,
her foot is a tapping piston.
And still the tracks spear the horizon—
    there, where a life floated up.

At Buckingham Palace, I think of Jon M

June 2007

Two guards shoulder their M16s—a rhyme of metal—
and the flag above the Queen snaps like gunfire.
But I'm not thinking about this place
or the tourists that surround me.
I'm remembering home, and one of my students.

Jon M has decided to put down a pen
and pick up the spitting sword of an M16.
He's off to Baghdad where all my teachings
will get blown to pieces beneath a date palm.

I think about thumping him on the chest
and saying, as I did at graduation,

   "You be *safe*."

Of what use is chalk compared to bullets,
how are my lessons on poetry going to save him now?
Maybe, beneath the ellipsis of illumination rounds,
or after a smoky exclamation point

   an explosion

one that rises gently into the sky,
   dropping commas and wet asterisks
deep into his imagination,
   maybe after heavy footnotes
punch the street,

then, poetry might be of use to him,
but not now, not today.

Today, words are just hot air,
as untouchable as a soul.

Meeting Terri for Lunch

Little Dean's Yard, Westminster

First,
we drifted back to college.

        Pine trees spike the lake,
        professors glide
        beneath an abbey banner,
        it is the early 1990s,
        and we are playing hooky,
        biting our nails over final grades.

In the library of Westminster School,
where she now works, we whisper about the past
as students whittle us down with their eyes.

When did this happen,
our sleepwalk into authority?
How did we become so old,
she the librarian, me the poet?

These students dare not ask for silence,
but they'd like to know why two drips
are bubbling in such a wasteland.

We could be outside now
swinging our cricket bats,
driving our Ferrari to a rock concert,
or playing video games,

but instead

we are giggling in a library
like two more useless adults.

Letter to James Joyce

London, June 16

Dear James,

Sorry I couldn't be in Dublin today
but I met up with your friend, Leopold Bloom.
After breakfast, we bought some lemon soap
and decided to watch "Trooping the Colour"—
can you believe that royal ceremony was <u>today</u>, of all days?
The Queen sat like a siren on the rock of her throne,
her guards pounded pounded pounded the air with drums,
their eyes were clamped behind steel helmets.
I swear it woke the dead in Westminster Abbey.

We left early (we were more interested in lunch)
and got cheddar sandwiches on Fleet Street,
then it was off to Waterloo Bridge to feed the gulls.
We were going to scoot into the British Library
for an exhibition on Shakespeare and Hamlet,
but Bloom dragged me into one pub after another.
We sailed drunkenly through the red lights of Soho,
saw men act like pigs, then stumbled back to Bloomsbury.
We rested at a cabman's shelter in Great Russell Square,
talked briefly about the waterworks system in London,
and Bloom treated me to a cup of hot chocolate.
Then we peed beneath the stars.

So James, even though I wasn't in Dublin today,
you should know that my feet are swollen with blisters,
and that when I finally crawled into bed,
I intoned your words: "He rests. He has travelled."

Sorry I missed the big day,

Patrick

The Same is Different Every Day

A fisherman in Galway once told me
the sea is different every day,
and this truth baptises me
whenever I navigate London.

If we learn a city well enough,
our ghost lives on every corner,
time becomes a pool,
and we submerge ourselves

again and again,
pearl-diving for streetsigns.
On mighty rivers of asphalt,
my restless feet hopscotch through time,

neither here, nor there.

Taking Photographs for Strangers

It happens near famous landmarks.
They offer their cameras, I take each one
like a keyhole. I put it to my eye,
and spy into their world.

With a fingerclick,
I pour amber onto the earth—
birds are in mid-flight, water stops,
a nugget of sunlight jewels a window.
I slot everything into place,
pieces are puzzled into a frame.

And when these tourists fly home,
part of me goes with them
to far off lands I will never see.
Long after this memory abandons me,
when it skips into the fog,
they will still have a snapshot
of a world I once saw.

What a strange gift.

They can crawl inside my eye,
point at the dazzling world,
and they can see everything,
exactly as I have forgotten it.

Outside the British Library

What happens to our memories
when the great pulse

        stops.

Is it like a candle
tipping over in Alexandria,

the papyrus of our lives
just blackened smoke—

or do we ascend into a library,
one with a glass dome,

wingback chairs,
each book a garden of ink?

In this afterworld
librarians mend broken spines,
they point to shelves of light,
and store our pain

        deep
    in the basement,
      down where the spiders grow.

Dictionaries are swollen,
plump, ripe with energy.
Only one word is censored:
that four-lettered obscenity, *shhh*.

So we author ourselves,
turning the heavy pages,
the calligraphy of our souls
      —scratched—
into woodpulp and rags.

Our stories may not be written to last,
but let us embrace the unknown,
let us open our arms like a book.

Note to a Friend Yet to be Born

If you think of me at all from your future,
I must seem like a tourist to you,
my antique clothes are not of your world.

Time may separate us,
but take this poem and know that,
if it weren't for an ocean of days between us,

I would invite you to a leafy park
where we could watch the clouds,
and compare notes on the city we love.

But, given enough time, you will join me,
and these streets which you currently command,
these buildings you hustle past, will all be given to another.

Then we—for, my friend, we will become "we"—
we can chuckle and watch them hold what once was ours …
these bricks, these landmarks, this gurgling river.

Love Song

The city crouches beneath the dawn, cool air rumbles through Moorgate, Rotherhithe, Camden, and Brixton. Oh London, you glow with shaking leaves and empty streets. Big Ben ripples the air, vowelstruck. Each wave of the tongued clapper swells the world. *Bing, bong, bang, bung…bung, bong, bing, bang.*

A newspaper waltzes through a park, it dances with a statue as blood pumps through a million waking hearts. When cars hive through your dirty honeycomb they lift the pistons of music, and I am tugged from the night by seagulls calling out their ancient chorus.

You are a city of ghosts. Footsteps hug your streets.

Sometimes it feels that my neighbour could be a medieval washerwoman, or a Roman centurion, their eyes are crusted with sleep, their thoughts honeyed with worry for their children. Like me, they might wonder about your first citizen, the one who decided to build a campfire among the mucky reeds, there, beside a river of stars.

Where was that first home, that first dawn?

No matter, today I am your beginning,
and I stretch my arms into you, once again.

Notes

ZONE 1.
The epigraph is from *Richard II* (Act II, Scene I).

THE POET OF LIVERPOOL STREET STATION.
Joseph Merrick (1862-1890) was a ward at the Royal London Hospital after he left the freakshow business. He was known as the "Elephant Man" due to a disease, probably neurofibromatosis, which he contracted at birth. His right arm, leg, and most of his skull was swollen to twice normal size. Dr Frederick Treves gave Merrick a room where he became something of social phenomena. We have no surviving record of Merrick's original poetry. For more information see Michael Howell and Peter Ford's *The True History of the Elephant Man* (1980).

LONDON UNDERGROUND.
While the Thames is the most visible waterway in London, a number of smaller rivers flow beneath the city. The Ravensbourne, Beverley Brook, Wandle, Fleet, and Westbourne still empty into the Thames but they have been captured in pipes. Part of the Westbourne can be seen in a massive cylinder that runs above the tube stop at Sloane Square. See Stephen Smith's *Underground London* (2004).

RIDING THE TUBE.
Each year more than 130,000 objects are left behind on the Underground. The items listed in this poem are some of the more unusual things that were forgotten in 2003. See Jo Swinnerton's *The London Companion* (2004).

RIDING THE TUBE AFTER THE BOMBINGS.
On 7 July 2005, 52 people were killed and 770 injured in a coordinated attack by four suicide bombers. Three Underground trains were destroyed as well as one bus in Tavistock Square. Twenty-four hours earlier, London was celebrating the announcement they would host the Olympics in 2012.

BURQA.
Edith Cavell (1865-1915) was a nurse in the Great War and executed by the Germans. These words, reportedly her last, are on a statue to her memory on Charing Cross Road. She believed all wounded soldiers have a right to medical attention regardless of nationality or political belief.

ZONE 2.
Epigraph from James Boswell's *Life of Samuel Johnson* (1791). Reportedly said by Johnson on 20 September 1777.

DICTIONARY.
Samuel Johnson's comprehensive *Dictionary of the English Language* was published in 1755 after nine years of work. Although it was not the first dictionary, it became the most popular and it made Johnson rich.

BATTERSEA POWER STATION.
This abandoned coal-fired electrical plant is now protected by the government. Built in 1939, it remains one of the largest brick buildings in Europe.

BEDLAM.
Bethlem Royal Hospital dates back to 1247. The building mentioned in this poem was a mental institution from 1815-1930. In the early years, the insane were usually outcasts and the public came to view them as a form of entertainment. The Imperial War Museum, established in June 1920 to honour the dead of the Great War, moved into this derelict building in 1936 where they have remained ever since. The mock trench mentioned in the second part of this poem is a popular display that recreates trench life in World War I. My thanks to the staff at the IWM for their patience and unerring kindness over the years.

AT THE GALLOWS OF TYBURN.
The condemned of Newgate Prison were hanged at Tyburn (now Marble Arch), which was a two-hour parade through London. The gallows were demolished in 1783 but at its busiest 24 prisoners could be executed at once. An estimated 65,000 people were hanged here, many for crimes we would consider petty today. "Tyburn Fair" was a raucous event full of drinking,

dancing, fornicating, and other festivities. See Roy Porter's *London: A Social History* (1994).

ZONE 3.
Epigraph taken from Oscar Wilde's *A Woman of No Importance* (1893).

LIGHTING THE CHRISTMAS TREE.
Every year since 1947, Norway has given the United Kingdom a massive spruce tree in gratitude for their sacrifices during World War II. The lighting ceremony in Trafalgar Square has become a popular holiday tradition.

THE LADY WITH THE LAMP.
Florence Nightingale (1820-1916) was a nurse in the Crimean War where she helped the wounded at Scutari. Nursing was not a respectable profession for women but Nightingale was determined to change public perception as well as care for patients.

IN PEACE.
The Grave of the Unknown Warrior is located at the entrance of Westminster Abbey. This is the first "unknown" to be honoured on behalf of other missing soldiers; he was laid to rest in 1920 and the grave is one of the most hallowed in the Abbey. At the time this manuscript was completed, the last British veteran of the Great War was 111-years-old and there was talk of burying his ashes next to this anonymous soldier. My thanks to Ian Godfrey at Westminster Abbey. Part two of this poem takes place at Charing Cross Station where many soldiers left for the Western Front. It is now a commuter rail station but during the war it was the scene of many final goodbyes. Part three of this poem takes place at the Imperial War Museum.

GENERATIONS AFTER THE PLAGUE.
The Black Death killed half of England between 1347 and 1350. Plague pits exist beneath the city and the virus, known as *pasteurella pestis*, remains a biological hazard to anyone who comes in contact with the dead. Whenever these corpses are exhumed during construction work (either accidentally or on purpose) they are carted away, cleaned, and stored in boxes. My thanks to Tim Morley at the Museum of London.

THE GREAT STINK OF 1858.
During the summer of 1858 the River Thames was so polluted that an unholy smell emanated throughout the entire city. Benjamin Disraeli described the choking air in the famous quote which begins this poem. The stink was so overpowering that plans for a modern sewage system were begun almost immediately. See Stephen Halliday's *The Great Stink of London* (1999).

THE KNOWLEDGE.
Quote taken from Robert Southey's *Letters from England* (1808). In order to prove they have memorised all the streets, London taxi drivers must pass a comprehensive test known as "The Knowledge". According to neurological studies this often leads to stimulated growth in their hippocampus, that part of the brain which is associated with memory.

ZONE 4.
Taken from *Collected Letters of W.B. Yeats*, vol. 1, ed. John Kelly (1986); letter dated August 25, 1888 to Katharine Tynan.

LONDON BURNING.
Over the past 2000 years London has suffered a series of fires and three of these reduced major portions of the city to ash. The first was started by Boudicca (also spelled Boadicea), who was queen of the indigenous Iceni people. When her husband died the Romans raped her daughters, banished her to the woods, and never expected to hear from her again. She returned to Londinium in 60 AD with an army of 100,000 and torched the city. The fire was so devastating that a band of red clay can still be found in the soil of London. The second significant blaze occurred in 1666. The mayor, Thomas Bludworth, was awoken when a fire started in Pudding Lane on the morning of 2 September. He reportedly said the line which begins section two of this poem. The conflagration lasted three days and reduced most of the city to powder. The Nazi bombing campaign of 1940–1941 destroyed wide areas of the map. The Blitz killed some 20,000 people but in spite of the mounting death toll and the utter ruin of their homes Londoners thickened their resolve to fight Hitler. The gravestone mentioned in this poem (Resurgam) is the actual cornerstone of Saint Paul's Cathedral and, miraculously, the

church remained undamaged throughout World War II. I have taken some poetic license with Churchill's quote; I suspect he asked this question but have no proof. For more information on all of the above see Roy Porter's *London: A Social History* (1994) and H.V. Morton's classic, *In Search of London* (1951).

INFAMOUS.
During the autumn of 1888 a man murdered five prostitutes in Whitechapel and Spitalfields. The killer drank at a pub called the Ten Bells which still stands today. The victims—Polly Nichols, Annie Chapman, Elizabeth Stride, Catherine Eddows, and Mary Kelly—were attacked with such brutality it shocked London. The identity of Jack the Ripper remains a mystery. Aside from various sources on the murders themselves, see Blanchard Jerrod and Gustave Doré's *London: A Pilgrimage* (1872) which captures the poverty of Whitechapel before the killings began.

ZONES 5-6.
Quote taken from Sam Selvon's novel, *The Lonely Londoners* (1956).

THINKING OF MY WIFE IN SOUTH DAKOTA.
Epigraph taken from V.S. Naipaul's "Two Thirty AM" (1964).

AT BUCKINGHAM PALACE, I THINK OF JON M.
This has been the London residence of the sovereign since 1837. The "Changing of the Guard" is a popular tourist attraction full of military pomp.

OUTSIDE THE BRITISH LIBRARY.
Tracing its roots to 1753, the British Library is a treasury of books. Among its 15 million items are: the Lindisfarne Gospels, *Magna Carta*, a copy of *Beowulf*, *The Canterbury Tales*, Leonardo da Vinci's notebooks, scribbled papers from the Beatles, James Joyce, Virginia Woolf, and Shakespeare. The memories of the dead, at least in this place, are alive and well.

Author Biography

Patrick Hicks is a dual citizen of Ireland and the United States, as well as Writer-in-Residence at Augustana College. He is the author of several poetry collections, including *Finding the Gossamer* (Salmon, 2008), and his work has appeared in scores of journals such as *Ploughshares, Tar River Poetry, Glimmer Train, Virginia Quarterly Review, Natural Bridge, Indiana Review, Nimrod*, and many others. Aside from being a Visiting Fellow at Oxford, he has been nominated several times for the Pushcart Prize and he is the recipient of a number of grants, including one from the Bush Foundation to support his first novel, which is about Auschwitz. After living in Europe for many years, he now enjoys thunderstorms rolling across Midwest America.